Helping Your Hurting Teen

H. NORMAN WRIGHT

AspirePress

Torrance, California

AspirePress

Helping Your Hurting Teen
Copyright © 2014 H. Norman Wright
All rights reserved.
Aspire Press, an imprint of Rose Publishing, Inc.
4733 Torrance Blvd., #259
Torrance, California 90503 USA
www.aspirepress.com

Register your book at www.aspirepress.com/register

The views and opinions expressed in this book are those of the author(s) and do not necessarily express the views of Aspire Press, nor is this book intended to be a substitute for mental health treatment or professional counseling.

Printed in the United States of America
010914RRD

Contents

CHAPTER ONE

Navigating the Turbulent Teen Years

A dolescence is a life phase characterized by turbulence and filled with an abundance of changes. This time between childhood and adulthood is filled with physical, mental, and emotional changes that can leave both you and your teen spinning. When adolescence hits, there are changes that will leave you scratching your head in bewilderment:

> ➢ The child who loved to talk to you is now a stranger who responds to you as if you're from outer space.

➢ Communication changes from talking and joking to sullen or ashen silence.

➢ Your teen's room becomes his or her cave. Your teen wants privacy, sleep, and escape from adults.

➢ Gadgets are your teen's life—smartphones, tablets, and anything associated with his or her computer.

➢ Mood swings and an overreliance on his or her peers are to be expected, and your teen's dress code will baffle you.

➢ Your teen won't want to be seen with you. Parents are an embarrassment to the teen. The teen thinks the ways his or her parents talk, act, and dress have changed for the worse.

➢ Most importantly, when your child becomes a teen, his or her intelligence increases. Just ask! Your teen seems to know almost everything there is to know. And your teen's friends' intelligence increases, too, which makes your job much harder.

One author describes the process that takes place during adolescence this way:

> Although there is no specific evidence to back this theory, it seems as if the energy that is required for the child to develop physically during adolescence seems to be drained directly from the parent's brain. The end result is that we lose IQ points and become less intelligent than when the child was nine or ten years old. Because of this loss in intelligence, our logic and reasoning become faulty. We approach life and the world from a very limited capacity, and our ability to adequately provide information and direction is significantly reduced. In other words, we get dumber and do not know what we are talking about.[1]

At least that's the way the teen sees parents! Mark Twain put it this way: "When I was a boy of 14, my father was so ignorant I could hardly stand to have the old man around. But when I got to be 21, I was astonished at how much the old man had learned in seven years."

In the book *The Eight Seasons of Parenthood*, the season of adolescence is called the volcano years. It's unpredictable. It's never dull. As a parent you're personally challenged by the change on all levels— physically, spiritually, intellectually, and emotionally.[2]

Adolescence is a roller-coaster experience—a time of stress and storm. Some teens have an easier time through these rocky years, but for many, adolescence is a time of continual crisis with a few respites in between. This is the time when self-doubt and feelings of inferiority are intensified and when social pressures are at their peak. Mood swings, discovering porn, trying alcohol, hanging out with bad friends, trouble with the law, lying, being disrespectful, ditching school, sneaking out at night—these are only a few symptoms telling you there are deeper things going on with your teen. It's important to realize that the teen years are filled with loss, sometimes on a daily basis. And it may seem like a low-grade fever of grief accompanies each adolescent through life.

TEENS AND LOSS

Many of the "volcanic" responses of teens stem from loss, which must be seen from their perspective, not the parents'. Rejection by another, losing an athletic event, having to wear braces at sixteen, and the like are definite losses to an adolescent. In turn, grief is a part of loss, although the type of grief will differ with the type of loss.

When adolescents lose a parent in death, they often deny it in order to protect themselves from this threatening experience and the ensuing feelings. If adolescents lose a friend in death, there is a strong anxiety. Teens are aware that adults die, but the death of a peer is shocking. It's unnerving. They have to face their own mortality at an age when they're not prepared to do so.

Another loss that many adolescents face is the divorce of their parents. When this occurs, there's a loss of security and confidence in the future. The divorce hampers the normal development of the adolescent for a period of time. Teens feel abandoned, and their need for strength from the family is disrupted.

A chronic, debilitating illness in a teen's family or circle of friends creates fear about the teen's own vulnerability. Even a friend's moving away brings a sense of loss. The pain suffered is as severe as rejection.

Symptoms of difficulty with handling losses include emptiness, fear, concentration problems, and fatigue. Teens may become critical. They may be afraid of talking about their pain, because they don't want to risk embarrassment for fear of having others see them as a failure. They often erupt in anger and rage.

IDENTITY CRISIS

Young people from thirteen to nineteen are becoming independent from their parents and at the same time experiencing a radical identity crisis. Many are able to establish their identity at this time, while others postpone this until adulthood.[3]

Professor of clinical psychology Les Parrott has identified several ways teens search for identity:

➤ *Family relations* have a significant impact on identity formation. Creating an identity within a family can come from other acceptable or unacceptable responses. Out-of-the-ordinary events, such as a disabled or drug-involved sibling, a family death, or a job loss, will also have an influence.

➤ *Celebrity idols* contribute elements to teen identity, but teens often tend to over-identify as they imitate the idol, thus seeming to lose their own individuality. Too often teen develop a blind adoration or devotion to someone who is famous and has abilities the teens wish they had. Idols do give teens an opportunity to test new behaviors and attitudes, but those often conflict with who the teen really are.

➤ *Cliquish exclusion* and the lack of tolerance for other people's differences also are part of the identity formation of teens and perhaps even a defense against identity confusion. And this is often where the problem of bullying arises.[4]

➤ *Status symbols* are another way to proclaim who they are. Friends, shoes, clothes, hairstyles, smartphones, electronics, cars, and so on add to who a teen is. But to be authentic, behaviors have to match the status symbol, which can lead to a reputation.

➤ *Grown-up behavior* is a part of the identity package, and many of these—smoking, drugs, sex, and drinking—are behaviors that teens are too young to deal with appropriately. Some of these behaviors are engaged in even before the teen years.

➤ *Rebellion* fits into the equation as well. It's a way for teens to attempt to resolve incongruent ideas and find authentic identity. Often this creates inner conflict.

➤ *Other people's opinions* also are essential. Teens need their self-image validated by others, especially other teens.

Eleven Breaking-Away Behaviors[5]

To be successful as an adult, teens need to move away from childhood dependence upon their parents. We call this movement "breaking away." But this move toward independence is stressful for parents, because they are not in control of how this movement develops. Let's look at the eleven normal breaking-away behaviors of teens that parents should be aware of:

1. Teens need quality time alone and with their peer group. They usually are neither eager for family get-togethers nor as interested in them as they used to be. To them a family get-together may be something that's tolerated.

2. Adolescents may withdraw from involvement, including church attendance. They tend to be secretive around their parents and don't confide in them like they used to as children. Those parents who have their children for their own identity,

needs, and self-esteem have difficulty handling this lack of confiding and wish for a return to the "good old days."

3. Teens are reluctant to accept advice or criticism from their parents. They're overly sensitive to suggestions, because their insecurities seem to arise when given advice or criticism. Their lack of properly formed identity and of low self-esteem tend to make them more sensitive at this time. They resent criticism. Discipline, criticism, and advice are interpreted as domination; and they feel out of control, and they need to be in control.

4. Rebellion is a common reaction. But the more secure the teenager, the less rebellion there is. The more insecure, the more radical the rebellion.[6]

5. During the late teenage years, allegiance and commitment are shifted more to individual peers of both the opposite and same sex. Teens may not want to be seen by their parents.

6. Teens' increased involvement with peers often creates anxiety for parents. Evenings spent talking on the phone or texting and a constant demand to be with friends are the norm. Changes in manners of dress, speech, musical tastes, enjoyable activities, and general behavior are usually related to the peer group.[7]

7. Adolescents often are absorbed with their own world but are limited by self-centeredness. They react in a subjective manner. If they are self-critical, they tend to assume others, including their parents, are also critical of them. They think of themselves as unique and special. They're satisfied with old friendships that sustain them rather than wanting to build new friendships. Moving to a new location at this time of life can be traumatic.

8. Social fears are high on the list of things teens are afraid of. They don't like feeling rejected, disapproved of, or ignored, nor do they want to look foolish or be out of control. Authority figures are among those to be feared.

9. The thinking process of teens is different from that of children. They recognize possibilities as well as actualities. They tend to over-idealize and think conceptually in abstract and universal terms. In addition to a search for personal identity, their strong sense of idealism creates anger and frustration. They know the way things should be and are intolerant when things are not that way. Their views on life's issues and values can fluctuate daily or by the hour.

10. Teenagers are overly dependent on feedback from their peers and may behave differently in different groups. Parents may wonder, *Who are they?*

11. When faced with an unexpected crisis, teens may lose the ability to see value in things. They become disillusioned, and when this occurs, they tend to become cynical and even degrade others. This all leads to a resistance to change that make counseling more difficult.[8]

COMMUNICATION HURDLES

Remember that during adolescence, communication usually decreases and teens confide less in their parents. This is normal, and parents should not take it personally. (Yes, there *are* exceptions, and you will hope your family is the exception).

With teens, listening is much better than logical arguments or retaliations. This is a time to listen for feelings and draw them out.

Teens hate it when they talk with their parents and don't have 110 percent of their attention. They need to see your face looking at them, so turn off the TV and computer and don't answer your cell phone.

Additionally, you have a greater chance of staying connected if most of what you say is positive rather than negative. Focusing on successes, accomplishments, and interests works better than focusing on mistakes and failures. One father asked his teen, "John, I don't like to talk about lapses or mistakes. Sometimes I need to. Tell me the best way to put it, and I'll follow that and keep it short. I'd much rather talk to you about what's working."

Finally, when you talk to your teen, use humor. Let him or her know that, because of your advanced age and sensitivity to distortion, you need to talk with your teen without the competition of the TV, music, or the Internet. You may even become sane as the conversation progresses. (It has worked for many!)

SEVEN TYPES OF LOSS

Many losses are more than a loss to a teen—they are so life-changing that they plunge a teen into the chaos of crisis or trauma. When your teen experiences a loss, the family experiences a loss. It affects everyone. When your teen experiences a crisis, the family experiences a crisis. And when your teen is traumatized, the whole family is traumatized. If the loss in a teen's life is a death, the whole family can feel chaotic and out of control. This is predictable and normal.

Another normal response is the feeling that your family will never feel normal or okay again. You will have to create a "new normal." This new normal accepts loss as a fact of life.

So far I've alluded to several kinds of losses. Losses actually fall into overarching categories, or types. I'll quickly group and identify at least seven, so you can watch for them in your teen's experience. As you read through the types of loss, think: *How have I experienced this type of loss in the past? What is—or will be—my teen's experience of it?*[9]

> When your teen experiences a crisis, the family experiences a crisis.

1. Material Loss

Material loss is a big one for any person. For a teen, it could involve the loss of a physical object or even familiar surroundings. The greater the attachment, the greater the sense of loss. A material loss is normally the first type of loss for children, or at least one they're aware of. It could be a broken toy or the fact that the dog ate their ice cream cone. These continue and multiply during the teen years.

The intensity of loss your teen feels is closely tied to the replaceability of whatever he or she lost. When your teen breaks a favorite piece of sporting equipment or smashes your car, the teen's sense of loss may subside in several days or weeks. But a pet dying will have a different impact. Unfortunately, many parents immediately provide the apparent solution: "We'll get you a new one." This is not the best approach. If the loss is replaceable, the replacement can mask grief, instead of helping the young person grieve and learn from the experience.

2. Relationship Loss

A relationship loss involves the end of the opportunity to relate to another person. Your teen will likely experience many of these events. When a friend isn't there, a teen can't talk with him or her, share experiences, touch, or even argue. This loss can result from a move, a divorce, or a death. It can also arise when having to face cliques in school, not wearing the right clothes, making or not making the team, or . . . just growing up.

3. Intrapsychic Loss

Intrapsychic is a fancy word to describe teenagers' self-perception when they experiences change. With loss, teens can lose an important emotional self-image. Not only that, teens also lose their sense of what they could have become in the future. The loss might force your teenager to change cherished plans or give up a longtime dream. Sometimes this loss occurs because of childhood—or even current—physical or emotional abuse that has impacted the teen emotionally and physically.

Often these plans and dreams have never been shared with others, so the loss that occurs is also a secret. Perhaps your son has his heart set on being a star player in high school and going on to be a major-league player. But he never learns to hit well enough, always being edged out by someone slightly better. Or your daughter wants to be a dancer or gymnast. But after six years of lessons, she shatters her leg or uncovers a physical defect. Now the loss involves much more than a batting average or a leg that is limber; it's intrapsychic as well. The person's vision of who he or she is—and will be—fades into the mist.

4. Functional Loss

We're all aware of the losses related to a muscular or neurological function of our bodies. They aren't relegated only to the old folks' home; they happen to teens, too. If possible, a teen will adapt or adjust, but some functional losses can be absolutely overwhelming. Accidents in sports or cheerleading can be devastating. Less visible problems such as genetic defects that result in hearing loss, limited heart function, and ADHD or bipolar disorder can create functional losses that are devastating.

When I was nine, I contracted polio. It was a light case, and even though I missed a semester of school, I suffered few aftereffects of the disease. Unfortunately, my doctors felt I shouldn't overdo, so I wasn't allowed to go out for sports. These losses required some adjustment time. Fortunately, I eventually put my energies into music and enjoyed some fulfilling experiences in that realm.

5. Role Loss

Role loss affects all of us. In a family, it's the loss of a certain accustomed place in the relationship network. The significance of the loss depends upon how much of the person's identity was tied into this role. For example, suppose an only child of thirteen starring at the center of family life has to share the room (and the family stage) with a new family member. The child is no longer the star player. Or imagine what happens when two families attempt to blend and become a stepfamily. With new stepsiblings, each teen now faces the task of taking up a transformed role. Since the old role is gone forever, it's a loss.

6. Ambiguous Loss

An ambiguous loss is a very difficult loss, and it comes in two prickly varieties. In the first type, family members perceive another member as physically absent but psychologically present, because it's unclear whether this person is dead or alive. It's the heartache of the missing soldier, a kidnapped child, or a runaway sibling. Will the absent person indeed return someday?

In the second type of ambiguous loss, a person is physically present but psychologically absent or mentally ill or abusive—a person with Alzheimer's disease, for example, or maybe a family member who has succumbed to addictions, making him or her numb to the family circumstances. When this happens in a teen's family, it is difficult for the teen to understand what's going on. It's not easy for a stepchild to handle the biological parent being excluded. Nor is it easy for a teen to constantly deal with a brain-injured dad who now functions like a five-year-old, or an addicted or emotionally dysfunctional parent who doesn't pay attention to the teen's needs.

Of all the losses experienced in relationships, an ambiguous one is the most devastating because it remains unclear, indeterminate. Perceiving loved ones as present when they are physically gone, or perceiving them as absent when they are physically present, the teen begins to feel helpless. Such loss makes any adult or teen more prone to depression, fear, anxiety, and ongoing relationship problems. It all leads to what is known as complicated grief.

7. *Threatened Loss*

One of the hardest losses of life is the threatened loss. The possibility is real, and there is little to do about it: a move, a divorce, a death, a job loss. As the possibility looms, the teen's sense of control withers away, and that loss of control hangs over the teen's head like a sword. It's the end of the world.

In surveying the kinds and types of losses that come into our lives, one thing becomes crystal clear: Nobody likes to suffer any sort of loss.

CRISIS AND TRAUMA[10]

Many of the losses teens experience are more than just losses. They're crises. A crisis is an event that disrupts the balance in a person's life to the extent that a person can't cope or function. With such an event, teens feel overwhelmed and can become immobilized. They suffer a temporary loss of coping. They're thrown off balance. They may be numb, can't think clearly, may experience a sense of panic, and usually feel out of balance. They don't know what to do, and their coping skills don't work.

With most crises, teens can recover without any lasting ill effects. But not when teens have experienced trauma. Trauma is the response to any event that shatters a person's safe world so that it's no longer a place of refuge. Trauma is more than a state of crisis. It is a normal reaction to abnormal events that overwhelm a person's ability to adapt to life and that leave him or her feeling powerless. Trauma disconnects the functioning of the two sides of the brain. The left side of the brain, the thinking part, contains words that clarify what happens in the right side of the brain, which is the emotional side. In a trauma, the two sides do not work together.

If you've ever been to a rodeo, you've probably seen a rider pursuing a steer. He guides his horse to that galloping steer and, at the precise moment, leaps from his horse, grabs the steer's horns, and pulls the animal to a dusty halt. With the right amount of pressure at the right time, he literally throws that steer to the ground. When you experience trauma, you're thrown about like that steer. Your world turns wild, out of control, and crazy.

What used to be seen as a safe world is no longer safe. What used to be seen as a predictable world is no longer predictable.

Trauma is emotional wounding. You feel, *I can't get over it*. You can be so assaulted that your beliefs about yourself and about life, your will to grow, your spirit, your dignity, and your sense of security are damaged. Teens end up feeling frightened and helpless. They can experience this feeling to some degree in a crisis and still bounce back, but in a trauma, they have difficulty bouncing back.

As the result of trauma, something happens in your brain that affects the way you process information. It affects how you interpret and store the event you experienced. In effect, it overrides your alarm system.

The trauma event is tattooed on the brain. I once worked with twenty-two high school students who witnessed a classmate shot by another student. Those students were traumatized by this event. Many lived in fear for months. Loud noises, the smell of gun powder, a boy with reddish hair (like the shooter), the sight of guns, walking alone, and being home alone were enough to trigger fear and tension.

Trauma symptoms (which are some of the symptoms of Post Traumatic Stress Disorder) include the distortion of time (time seems longer or shorter than the actual length of the incident), fixation of attention, hyper-vigilance, negative hallucination (not seeing or hearing what's going on right in front of them), intrusive thoughts, flashbacks, and age regression (talking or acting as they did years before). The only benefit with time distortion might be that teens might not see or remember all the mayhem around them.[11]

If your teen experienced a trauma as a young child or as a recent event, he or she may need counseling.[12]

TEENS AND FEAR

Today's teenagers fear many things: physical violence such as shootings, stabbings, gang fights, and bullying; and psychological violence such as verbal harassment, racism, and intolerance. They also fear failing tests, not getting into college, and not being a part of the "in group." Teenage girls fear not being pretty, not having the right body, and not having the right clothes or friends. Teenage boys fear not being cool, not having the right clothes, not having the right body type, not making the team, not being comfortable talking with girls, and not having the right car. Teens at "wealthy" schools and teens at "poor" schools share many of these fears.

All teens have some fears. Make sure that these are normal fears, such as fear of failing, fear of not being able to live up to one's heroes physically or mentally, fear of bullying or other physical violence, and fear or abuse or rejection from parents, friends, teachers, or peers.

Know your teen's fears. Have a relationship in which your teenager feels free to tell you almost everything.

Show by your words and actions that your teenager can talk to you about things that really worry him or her. Don't preach or yell, and don't disparage your teen's fears. Don't tell your teen that he or she is being silly. Listen with sympathy and empathy and without judgment. Encourage your teenager to talk openly with you. Listen more than you talk. Give advice only when asked for it.[13]

Dr. Richard Heyman, professor of communication and education (and parent to three now-grown children), has suggested several things to say and do in order to help your teen handle fears:

Your teen's fears are real regardless of how they seem to you. Treat them as real. Take them seriously. Say such things as:

➢ You seem worried. Are you concerned about something?

➢ I know something's bothering you. Want to talk about it?

➢ What's happened to make you feel like this?

Use words that show that you want to help. Say such things as:

➤ Is there anything I can do?

➤ I want to help you, but I can't if you won't tell me what's wrong.

➤ We're all behind you if you need us.

Accept your teen's fear as completely reasonable for him even if you think it is unreasonable. Offer your help in working things through. Say such things as:

➤ You have got to work this out, and I'm here to help.

➤ Tell me the problem, and let's see if we can come up with some solutions.

➤ I know you're scared, and you have every right to be. But here's another perspective on this.

Suggest a systematic approach to dealing with fear. Say such things as:

➤ How about writing down what's bothering you

so we can look at it together?

➢ Let's write down the worst-case scenario and then the best one to get a better handle on things.[14]

You could also say:

➢ I may not have the answers, but I can find a specialist who can help us.

➢ Let me do some research and let's see how other people have solved this problem.

➢ When I pray for you, what would you like me to pray about?

THE CRISIS OF DEATH

Although how parents can help their teen handle death will be discussed in much more detail in the next chapter, some general remarks should be made here.

Teens may react to a major loss or death like adults, or their grief may resemble that of a child. With a family death, teens may separate even more from other family members and become enmeshed in other activities or other people. Development may come to a halt for a while. Teens may even start acting younger than normal for a period of time. Either teens will have difficulty resolving the loss long term, which blocks their continuing development, or over time they will develop greater maturity and growth.

What do adolescents need at a time of major loss? Security. Safety and security are major needs. Remember that what teens know is probably going to be different from what they feel. If a parent or the main adult in their life dies, they may feel abandoned. Teens appear much more mature than they are. They need to know someone is there for them physically, emotionally, and spiritually. They need to know that other family members are available.

They also need intimacy. If the one who died—whether it be a parent, sibling, close friend, or pet—loved them unconditionally, a major hole in their life has appeared.

They also need connection with the one who died. Mary Ann and James Emswiler, the founders of The Cove (a program for grieving children) and the New England Center for Loss and Transition, said:

> It may be critical to his emotional wellbeing that he remain attached until he can move away on his own. If he is in the process of separating, he may hold on to the memory of the dead parent so that he can break away from him and continue the development process. The parent may die, but the anchor remains.[15]

The act of separation needs to be done in a healthy way. The sharing of feelings is necessary. If at all possible, grieving teens should be enrolled in a teen support group; if one isn't available, parents should consider starting one.

Teens also need to find some relief from their emotional pain. Their secure world has crumbled. Many teens who abuse alcohol or drugs or act out aggressively are actually trying to relieve the pain from some loss.

And whenever possible, it's important for adolescents to get back on track developmentally. They'll have to do it without some of the resources they had before, but they can learn to cope.

Dr. Richard Heyman has suggested several things to say and do in order to help your teen handle death:

> If your teen's friend is dying or dead, encourage your teen to express his anger, his frustration, his sorrow, and sometimes his guilt. Death disrupts the normal, taken-for-granted flow of everyday life. Help your teen put it into a normal context. Say such things as:
>
> ➤ Would you like to talk about _____?
>
> ➤ I've had friends die, and I know how hard it is.
>
> ➤ It's hard to understand why these things happen. But let's talk.
>
> If the death seems to be affecting your teen seriously, encourage him to talk to [someone] who has extensive experience helping people cope with

the death of someone close. Say such things as:

➤ Do you think you'd like to talk to [member of the clergy]?

➤ I'm going to ask _____ if s/he would come over on Sunday, so we can talk about this.

➤ You may not like this, but I'm going to make an appointment for you to see Dr. _____. I think you need someone with more experience [in the area of grief and loss] than I have to help you through this. . . .

If your teen has lost a parent, grandparent, sibling, or any other close relative, you need to let him see you grieve. Show him that it's all right to cry, to be sad, to be angry, to not understand. Above all, encourage him to express his feelings openly and not hold them in. Talk to him about the person, about the good things in her life. Help him understand that acceptance is easier after they have been grieving. But don't expect things to happen overnight. It can take months or years. Say such things as:

- I know you miss _____ terribly. So do I.

- It's okay to cry. Your tears are a tribute to the love you had for _____.

- It's okay to ask why. You may never get a clear answer, but it's okay to ask.

- Death is always hard, even when it's an older person.

- We'll miss her, but she'll always be there in our memories.

- Take your time getting through this. Don't try to shut out what happened. Don't try to make sense of it either. It's just one of those things in life that happens whether we want it to or not. Even though you can't believe it right now, time will heal you.

Encourage your teen to attend the funeral or memorial service. Whether it's for a friend, parent, or relative, it's very important for the teen to participate in this grieving ceremony. Talk to him about it if he has never been to one before. Help him see the importance of communal grieving and saying goodbye. Say such things as:

➤ Do you want to go to the service? It's a good way to say goodbye.

➤ Do you know what happens at a funeral or memorial service? Let me describe it for to you.[16]

You could also say:

➤ My favorite memory was _____. What's yours?

➤ Would you like to say something at the funeral or write a card or a note?

➤ Would you like to write down your favorite memory with _____?

Here are some Scriptures you could also share with your teen: Psalms 4:8; 31:10, 14–15; 73:26; 94:14; 116:8-9; 119:28; Isaiah 41:10; John 16:20.

CHAPTER TWO

Helping Teens Handle Loss

E very loss requires some amount of grieving, but some teens have trouble grieving.[17] It's important to identify what may inhibit teens' ability to grieve the losses they experience, so that grieving does take place. The following factors most often inhibit grieving:

> ➤ The parents are not good at grieving. They have had difficulty grieving past or current losses.

> ➤ Parents are unable to handle and accept their children's expressions of painful experiences and try to ignore them. The parents do not know how to respond.

➤ The teens are worried about how the parents are handling the loss. In some cases teens attempt to protect the parent.

➤ The teens are overly concerned with maintaining control and feeling secure and may feel frightened or threatened by grieving and especially the vulnerability of crying in front of others.

➤ Parents don't caringly encourage their teens to grieve.

➤ The teens don't have the security of a loving, caring environment.

➤ In the case of a loved one's death, teens may question their role in making it happen. Their misplaced guilt is further enhanced if they have ambivalent feelings toward the loved one.

➤ Parents or other key family members might have a hard time accepting the reality of the death or other loss. The family fails to acknowledge and discuss the reality of death or loss.[18]

SEVEN STEPS IN THE GRIEVING PROCESS

Regardless of the type of loss teens experience, the following seven steps are important in the grieving process:

1. Teens need to accept the loss, experience the pain, and express their sorrow.

2. They may require assistance to identify and express the wide range of feelings they're experiencing. Encourage them to talk, write, or draw their feelings.

3. They need to know why others are sad and why they themselves are sad. Acknowledging these feelings lets them know that it's *okay* to be sad. Tell them, "This is how we feel when someone dies."

4. Teens must be told that it is the death that has made people sad, not the response or lack of response of the teens. Without an explanation, teens may think others' responses are caused by something they did or didn't do.

5. In the case of a death, teens need encouragement to remember and review their relationship with the loved one.

6. Teens need help in learning to relinquish and say goodbye to as well as talking about what they lost.

7. Teens respond differently to loss depending on their age and level of emotional maturity.

REACTIONS TO THE DEATH OF A LOVED ONE[19]

Carol Staudacher, author and grief consultant, has described a variety of reactions that are common for teens to experience when a loved one dies.

Fear

Teens who experience the death of a loved one can experience a number of additional fears, including the following:

➤ *Fear of losing the other parent, siblings, or grandparents*—Teens tend to see the remaining people as candidates for death.

➤ *Fear of their own death*—This is especially true if the teens are younger than the person who died or is approaching the age at which the person died.

➤ *Fear of going to sleep because they equate sleep with death*—Even the childhood prayer that begins "If I should die before I wake" reinforces this misconception. Dreams and nightmares intensify the fear.

➤ *Fear of separation because of the perceived insecurity of the home and family*—Teens no longer feel safe and protected. They're hesitant to talk about their feelings because it may upset the other family members. One girl told me, "When Dad died, I wanted to talk to my mother about it. But I was afraid to because it made her cry, and I didn't want the others yelling at me 'cause I did that. So I stuffed my feelings."

Guilt

The second feeling associated with grief is guilt. It's difficult to identify all of the sources of guilt, but there seem to be three main reasons teens experience guilt when a loved one dies:

1. "He [or she] died because I did something wrong. I screwed up!" Teens have a knack for remembering things they've done that they think are wrong. They may have made a mistake, broken something, or forgotten to say or do something. Just like adults, teens can end up with an incredible list of if-only thoughts, or regrets. But they may not verbalize these to their parents.

2. "I wanted him [or her] dead, I thought it, and it happened." Sometimes when these thoughts are persistent, teens wonder if somehow these negative thoughts had an effect. They worry about others finding out.

3. "I didn't do what I should have." Guilt may occur over misbehavior, not sharing or showing their love for them or not being the child their parents wanted them to be.

Anger

Another common grief response is anger. A number of beliefs trigger this reaction. Teens often feel abandoned and left to face life on their own. They're angry because their future has been dramatically changed—they won't be with that special person anymore. The death messed up their plans. They feel victimized by events that are out of their control.

Teens may be angry at their parents for several reasons:

> Not telling them that the person who died was so sick.

> Spending so much time with the sick person (they feel neglected and isolated).

> Just needing someone to be angry with.[20]

Teens express their anger in different ways. It may be targeted like a well-aimed bullet or sprayed in all directions like shotgun pellets. It may be directed at family members, friends, teachers, pets, or even at God. It may be expressed in tantrums, fights, silent hostility, or verbal blasts. As difficult as it may be to experience these demonstrative expressions of anger, they are healthy signs. The alternative response—bottling up the anger—can result in digestive problems and depression.

Confusion

A sense of confusion can also accompany the loss of a loved one. Just imagine that you are a thirteen-year-old who was raised in a Christian home and your dad dies. You'd probably wonder, *Where is God? Why didn't he keep my dad alive? Why didn't he make him well? I prayed every day! My uncle told me Dad went to be with God. Why'd God do that?* Not only are teens confused about God, but they are dealing with a mixture of feelings about the person who died.

They're trying to sort through mixed messages and advice they receive from grown-ups. The expectations of adults also often create confusion. One adult may imply to a teenage boy, *Oh, you poor child. You must feel so sad and alone.* At the same time, another adult may be giving the message, *Now you're the man in the family. You'll have to be strong.* The teen will be confused by the conflicting messages that say to be strong, sad, in control, a help to others, and so on.

The memories of the deceased also can cause confusion. Teens may hear the survivors talk about the loved one in a way that conflicts with their memories. The survivors praise and laud the dead person's perfect abilities in a way teenagers cannot understand. They may wonder, *Was Dad really as perfect as they say? I didn't know that. Sometimes I didn't even like him, and I thought he was bad when he yelled and went on and on. Maybe I was wrong. I hope no one finds out what I think.* You can see how this would create confusion as well as guilt.

The fluctuating moods of others also can generate confusion. Individuals around the teens may be cheerful one moment and moody and quiet the next. While this is a normal response, teens at this time seek stability and assurance from these people, but their changing moods cause teens to question their own responses. A teen may think, *Was it me? Did I do something wrong? Do they want me around or not?*

ELEVEN STEPS FOR PARENTS TO USE WITH GRIEVING TEENS

1. Give Teens Permission to Grieve, and Encourage Them to Talk and Ask Questions

Whether the loss is the death of a family member, a major move or the loss of a pet, your teen needs permission to mourn. For certain kids, though, even permission may not be enough. Some need an invitation to share their feelings, but they also need to be taught how to express sorrow. A few sensitive, well-directed questions can draw them out. A statement like, "Sometimes what has happened is confusing. It's hard to put it into words. You may want to think about it and write down some questions to ask when you're ready. Just let me know."

One of the best tools to encourage conversation I've found to use with those of all ages is the Ball of Grief. This can help even the most uncommunicative teens open up and share. Give them (or the entire family) a copy of the drawing and have everyone use markers or crayons to identify what they're experiencing. It helps to describe how each one is experiencing this feeling. Some describe where they are experiencing this in their body and how it's affecting their daily life.

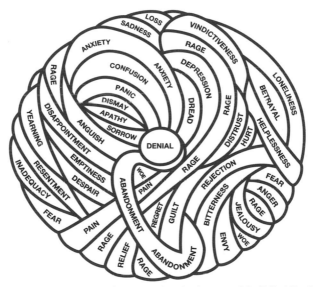

Go to www.hnormanwright.com to download copies of the Ball of Grief.

If they still do not talk, don't force it. Just let them know that you're available and ready to listen when they want to talk. You may wish to look for other ways for them to express what they're feeling.

I've used the Blob Tree with many, and I've seen the quietest teens become talkers.[21] All I do is ask them to select the blobs that represent them in their grief at this time and select the blobs that represent their other family members. We talk about who they are and what they're doing. How they respond can be different week by week and month by month.

Once teens begin to talk about their feelings, it may seem like you've untapped a gusher. They are—in their limited capacity—attempting to make sense of what has happened and regain their security. Teens whose questions are answered and who are given a forum for discussion have less need to fantasize and are much easier to help than those who are nonexpressive. If your teens don't share their feelings, watch for indirect questions or statements of concern and try to put their feelings into words for them.[22]

The Blob Tree

2. Be Available When They're Ready to Grieve

Being available may be the most important element in helping teens grieve. They need affection and a sense of security, although they may not admit this. Touching them and making eye contact will provide comfort and reassurance. Let them know that it is normal to have ups and downs. They're not going crazy. Help them break the mourning into manageable pieces so that they don't get overwhelmed. Using illustrations and word pictures can help them identify and talk about their feelings.

Teens need affection and a sense of security.

It helps to explain to them what grief is really like. This can help them normalize what they're experiencing. What some call the *crazy* feelings of grief are actually a *sane* response to grief. The following are all symptoms of normal grief:

➢ Distorted thinking patterns, "crazy" and/or irrational thoughts, fearful thoughts

- Feelings of despair and hopelessness

- Out of control or numbed emotions

- Changes in sensory perceptions (sight, taste, smell, etc.).

- Memory lags and mental "short-circuits"

- Inability to concentrate

- Obsessive focus on the loved one

- Losing track of time

- Increase or decrease of appetite and/or sexual desire

- Difficulty falling or staying asleep

- Dreams in which the deceased seems to visit the griever

- Nightmares in which death themes are repeated

- Physical illnesses like the flu, headaches, or other maladies

- Shattered beliefs about life, the world, and even God[23]

And you can add to the list:

➤ Increased irritability

➤ May want to talk a lot or not at all

Some parents are surprised to find that teens have the same range of emotions as they do. But teens need others to help them identify their feelings and the sources of those feelings, and express them in constructive ways, especially anger.

3. Answer Their Questions in Ways They Can Understand

Remember their age. Teens can't yet grasp what we can, and if we respond with an adult answer to a teen's question, they may not be able to handle it. And if they're in a state of shock or crisis, their thinking ability is lessened even more. It's important that when teens ask questions, they receive simple, concrete answers to what they've asked—if there are any answers. Sometimes all we can say is, "I wish I had an answer for you," or, "It doesn't make sense to me, either."

4. Give Them Opportunities for Creative Expression

Teens who have difficulty verbalizing their feelings may find it easier to express them on paper. Drawing is an effective way for them to gain control over their emotional pain and eventually eliminate it. When the loss is a death, drawing is especially important, because it allows them to actually see what their feelings look like. This action helps give them a sense of understanding and control.

Writing or journaling also is beneficial for those whose writing skills are developed. It is easier to express on paper the reality of what's happened and their fantasies about it. Writing a letter to the deceased person or even to God can be helpful. Encourage them to read their letters aloud and discuss what they've written, but remember to respect their privacy. The choice whether or not to share needs to be theirs. They may share more openly on social media (including such things as blogs) than in talking with you.

5. Create Opportunities for Breaks from Grieving

Periodically, teens need to be encouraged to take a break from their grief and interact with friends. Interacting with others is important for teens. In the safety of their peers, they vent various feelings. This helps them to regain a feeling of safety and security. It gives them a feeling of power over the effects of loss and allows them to separate themselves from what has happened.[24]

They may feel like they're betraying the deceased if they have fun or allow themselves some enjoyment. But interacting is a normal and beneficial part of their lives and gives them time to recuperate. It also helps them realize that life goes on. Encourage time with peers and adults. Let me give you a case in point:

In the early 1960s, I served on the staff of a church as a youth pastor and minister of education. Fresh out of seminary, I wasn't sure if I knew what to do. . . .

Each summer we took a group of students on an outreach or study outing. One year we took 25 high school students to the High Sierras in Southern California for several days. We camped in tents, biked, fished, talked, and studied together. Nearby was a formidable, massive rock formation—Crystal Crag—over 1,000 feet high. The sheer wall was a challenge to even the most skilled climber.

One morning two of the high school boys (one, a recent graduate who was waiting to go into the navy) decided on their own to climb the face of this cliff. They left before anyone was awake and did not inform anyone of their plans. . . .

It's still unclear how they were able to scale the rock face, given the lack of equipment and expertise, but they climbed for several hundred feet before Phil lost his handhold and plunged over 400 feet to his death. Every bone in his body was broken. . . .

I'll never forget that day. We all sat in small groups talking in hushed voices, feeling numb and stunned. We fixed dinner, and then, strangely enough, the group began to joke, cut up and laugh for the next hour. Other adults around us were bothered by their response. However, I realized later that this was their way of taking a break from the heaviness of the crisis. It was a normal response, because adolescents tend to move in and out of their grief.[25]

6. Watch Your Expectations

Everyone needs to be careful not to overprotect teens. Lecturing or making decisions for them isn't helpful while they're coping with a loss. When possible, it is better if they learn to make their own choices and are allowed to grow through the experiences of their lives. Sometimes parents become overrestrictive or overprotective.

The flip side of this issue, though, is that adults often have expectations that are inappropriate for the age level of teens. I've overheard parents or other adults say to a teen, "You're going to have to take over now and be the strong one." I've also heard, "You'll have to put sports and college on hold now." This is an unrealistic expectation and places too much of a burden on teens. These kinds of messages will short-circuit their grieving process. They need to be given age-appropriate responsibilities.

7. Help Them Separate Myths from Reality

Teens will often be impatient with themselves, because they feel sad longer than they think they should. They believe there is a time limit. They also feel that no one has ever felt the way they do, so they may be uncomfortable with their friends. They need to be told not to expect too much of themselves or others at this time and

Be careful not to overprotect teens.

that everyone grieves as long as they need to; they need encouragement to talk with their friends— especially those who have experienced similar losses. Communicating with others of all ages normalizes what they're experiencing.

To help teens normalize what they've been experiencing, go over with them the list of normal symptoms of grief (see #2). Sit down with your teen and together read through this list of the normal symptoms of grief. Ask your teen, "Which ones have you experienced? All of these are normal."

8. Make Honesty a Policy

While grieving, your teen may look to adults for hope and encouragement. When they ask adults questions (and hopefully they will), you need to avoid giving them platitudes and, instead, let them know it is all right to ask why when bad things happen.

Don't expect them to respond as adults.

This question is not just a question—it is a sign of protest as well. Let the protest occur, for many of the psalms contain this protest as well. You need to admit that you don't have all the answers—and may never have the answer to that question—but that you'll get through it together. One parent told her fifteen-year-old son, "I know it is a hard time for you. We are all sad and wish things were different. There are many changes happening right now, but in time things will settle down. Someday the pain will go away. It may go away gradually and keep returning again and again, but as we help and love one another, it is going to go away.[26]

When there's been a death, discuss whether or not this is their first experience with death. If it is, they will need help to understand the loss and sort out their feelings about it. Be especially sensitive to their reactions and anticipate the unexpected. Use words and phrases they can easily understand (it may help first to rehearse with someone else what you plan to say). And just because they may not say much doesn't mean they haven't been impacted.

9. Allow Them to Respond in Their Own Way

Don't expect them to respond as adults. Initially, some teens may not seem upset or sad. They even may have difficulty remembering the deceased. They may need help to remember their relationship with the deceased before they can resolve their grief. Photos and videos are helpful. Reminiscing about times spent together and reviewing certain qualities of the person may also be helpful.

Teens often regress (talk or act as they did years before) because they don't know how to grieve.[27] The important thing is for all of them to progress at their own rates. Adults need to be available to observe their reactions. If they begin to express strong feelings, encourage them—don't block them. Allow them to cry or express anger or even bitterness. Let them yell and stomp around. In time, they will probably begin to ask questions. Answer them simply and honestly, even though you may struggle with them yourself.

10. Watch for Signs of Fear

Teens need reassurance that their family still exists and that they are important parts of it. They may tend to ask the same questions over and over again. Their questioning may become intense as they attempt to assimilate what has happened and how it will affect their lives. You may need an abundance of patience to answer their questions again and again in a loving way.[28]

Teens will most likely become aware of their vulnerability to losing other important people or things as they evaluate how this loss will affect their lives. Anything of importance to them could become the object of fear. It may be their home, school friends, church, pets, a daily routine, an activity, or another loved one. They will require constant and consistent reassurance. It is important to discuss with them in advance if there are any planned changes in the future.

11. Encourage the Continuation of Normal Routines

It helps if teens continue certain family routines. Routines provide security and let them know there are certain constants in their lives—things they can rely on to stay the same. One of the most practical things to do is to encourage them to take good care of themselves—to get plenty of rest and exercise and to eat balanced meals.

CHAPTER THREE

Dealing with Anger and Depression

Regardless of the kind of loss a teen experiences—whether it's a death or an issue at school or a breakup with a girlfriend or boyfriend—there will be some intense emotions. Two of the most common responses to loss during adolescence are anger and depression.

TEENS AND ANGER

Your teen gets angry. But you already know that. Your teenager may have a lot to get angry about. Older kids may bully. Schoolmates may say things behind your teen's back or make him or her the butt of jokes. Teachers may say, "Stop doing that! What's wrong with you?" Others may not know how to respond to death or loss in your family. Your teen may think you don't understand: "I don't care what you promised your friend. No phone calls until you've finished your homework." Your teen may not know exactly who he or she is or where he or she is going. Your teen probably thinks he or she doesn't even control his or her own life. Anger is a natural reaction to all of this.

Don't be surprised if teens express anger at themselves. It may be rational, or it may not be rational. Some tend to take responsibility for all of their losses. God may also be the recipient of the blame and anger. Don't be threatened by this. Encourage teens to pray their anger toward God or to write God an angry letter. This can be an avenue for God to use to strengthen a teen's relationship with him. In time, the anger will subside.

Many parents want to know what they can do once their teen is angry. But that's not the place to begin.

The best time to help teens deal with anger is before they get angry.

One of the most helpful things you can do is to normalize the emotion of anger. Talk about emotions with your teen. Help your teen understand what emotions are and where they come from. Make sure your teen knows that emotions aren't good or bad, right or wrong. Let your kids know that you are encouraged when they identify their anger. This suggests that they are growing in their understanding of their emotions. It indicates that they are learning how to deal with this powerful emotion in healthy ways.

Remember, anger is always a response to another emotion or combination of emotions. Many factors can contribute to anger, but the primary causes are hurt, frustration, and fear.

> *Hurt* is usually caused by something that has happened in the past. It makes us feel vulnerable and open to further hurt. This is, especially true of very sensitive teens.

➤ *Frustration* is an emotion that takes place in the present. We become frustrated by blocked goals and desires and unmet expectations. It's especially easy for teens to become frustrated. Frequently, the things that cause frustration aren't very important, but they appear to be of major significance to teens.

➤ *Fear* is an emotion that tends to focus on the future. Many people associate fear with vulnerability and weakness.

➤ Anger can be destructive, but it can also be constructive. It's destructive when it hurts people or relationships. It's constructive when it is used for positive things, such as motivating one to work harder in school, deciding who one's real friends are, laughing at teasing, learning how to take and make jokes about oneself, and learning how to talk things through with parents or teachers who want to listen.

THREE THINGS TO DO FOR ANGRY TEENS

There are three main things you need to say and do when teens are angry:

1. *Understand* their anger.

2. Help them *manage* their anger.

3. Help them *channel* their anger into productive emotions and actions.

1. Understand Their Anger

If teens feel they have a sympathetic parent, they might offer information. If your teen is normally shy about talking with you, but you suspect anger about something, show your teen you're there for him or her. Say something like:

> ➤ You look angry. Is there anything wrong?

> ➤ I have a feeling that you're upset about something. Is it something I said?

➤ Whenever you talk that way, I know something is wrong. Would you like to talk about it?

➤ What do you mean you're not hungry? Is something upsetting you?

➤ I think something is bothering you. Why don't we sit down and talk for a while? Or if it's easier, write me a note and I'll read it.

If your teen is more upset with you and says, "I'm angry?" you could respond with:

➤ You *sound* angry. What happened to make you so mad?

➤ I know what you're feeling. I get angry, too. Tell me about it.

➤ Let's talk. You can tell me what's wrong.

Remember to listen, even when you don't like what is said or you feel your teen is wrong. Don't try to fix everything. Once you've begun talking, remember that you first want to *understand* the cause of the anger and how your teen is feeling about it.

Say something like:

- ➤ Talk to me.

- ➤ Look, I'm here for you. I'm not going to do anything but listen. So talk to me.

- ➤ I hate to see you upset. What's wrong? Think about it, and when you're ready to share, I'll listen.

- ➤ Do you trust me enough to tell me what happened?

- ➤ I don't want to pry, but I want to hear about what happened.

2. Help Them Manage Their Anger

Teens need help to manage their anger. Dwell on the positive. Try to relate their experience this time to other times they've been angry and how those situations were successfully handled, and to ways you cope with your own anger.

You could say such things as:

> ➢ I don't blame you for being so angry. I hated ninth grade, too. What could you do about it that won't make things worse?

> ➢ The last time you were so angry, do you remember what you did to get over it? How did it work? How did it make you feel?

> ➢ Here's what I do when I'm angry. It may help or it may not.

> ➢ Let's take this anger apart, look at what caused it, and then figure out what you can do about it.

> ➢ It's good to talk when you're angry. Tell me what you'd like to do.

> ➢ It may help to write an angry letter and then read it out loud.

3. Help Them Channel Their Anger into Productive Emotions and Actions

Once parents and teens understand the anger, teens need help channeling the anger into something positive. You could say such things as:

> ➤ What can you do to make sure it doesn't happen again?

> ➤ Which of these things would be best for you?

> ➤ If this happened to your sister [brother], how would you help her [him] deal with it? What advice would you give?

> ➤ In situations like this one, what can you control and what can't you control?

> ➤ Have you ever made someone else angry? How did you do it? Why did you do it? How did it make him [her] feel about you? Would you do it again?

SCRIPTURES ABOUT ANGER

Let's take a look at some of the Scriptures that talk about anger. The basic overall theme of Scripture concerning anger is that it will be part of life. It is not to be denied, but it is to be controlled.

Ephesians 4:26 tells us to "Be angry, and do not sin" (NKJV). This is one of the passages (along with Mark 3:5) where anger is legitimate. The word *angry* in this verse means an anger that is an abiding and settled habit of the mind and that is aroused under certain conditions. There is no revenge. The person is aware of this kind of anger, and it is under control. There is a legitimate reason for this anger.

The mind must be in control of the emotions so that the ability to reason is not lost. "Be angry, and do not sin." Perhaps the way this is accomplished is related to the scriptural teaching of Proverbs 14:29 and 16:32 to be "slow to anger" (NASB).

The Word of God also has something to say about suppressing or holding anger back:

> *"He who is slow to anger has great understanding, but he who is hasty of spirit exposes and exalts his folly."*
> — Proverbs 4:29, AMP

> *"Good sense makes a man restrain his anger, and it is his glory to overlook a transgression or an offense."*
> — Proverbs 19:11, AMP

> *"I [Nehemiah] was very angry when I heard their cry and these words. I thought it over and then rebuked the nobles and officials."*
> — Nehemiah 5:6–7 AMP

"I thought it over" has also been translated as "I consulted with myself" (KJV).

TEENS AND DEPRESSION

What does a depressed teen look like? How can parents know if their teen is really depressed and not just sad about something that has happened? You first need to understand the distinction between depression and sadness.[29] The feeling of sadness is less intense than that of depression; it doesn't last as long nor does it interfere with day-to-day functioning. Depression causes us to function at 50 percent of normal, and this lower functioning level intensifies our feelings of depression.

Depressed teens feel empty. They cannot fully understand the void within, but they know that something is wrong. Below are some possible symptoms. (Your teenager may not show all of these.)

1. A depressed teen may appear sad or depressed; this is called apathy and can be expressed in several ways. The teen might appear restless but doesn't become involved in activity, may decline to do things he or she usually enjoys, preferring to be

alone to just daydream. Apathy can be a symptom of internal stress.

2. The teen may exhibit listlessness and look bored or often even appear to be ill. The teen might lie around or walk aimlessly from place to place or room to room.

3. A depressed teen may display physical symptoms, often complaining of headaches, stomachaches, dizziness, insomnia, or eating and sleeping disturbances. These symptoms are called depressive equivalents.

4. The teen may look discontented and seem to experience very little pleasure from life.

5. Many feel rejected and unloved. They withdraw from any situation that may disappoint them. They fear and expect rejection and try to protect themselves from it.

6. They feel unimportant. The method or expression differs from teen to teen. These feelings of

inadequacy and low self-esteem may appear in the following ways:

➤ Quitting a club or sports team because he sees himself as insignificant. ("They'll never miss me.")

➤ Failing to reach out to help others for fear of rejection. ("She will think I'm a loser.")

➤ Rejecting affection because of a feeling of unworthiness. ("She can't really love me.")

➤ Deliberately breaking rules because he thinks following them will lead to failure. ("Others expect too much of me. They won't like it when I fail.")

➤ Failing to recognize that mistakes and failures can be corrected. ("I'll never get it right.")

➤ Refusing to admit to a mistake or failure to save face. ("Why do I always lose?")

➤ Rejecting the need to learn or grow. ("What difference will it make if I know that or not?")

> Unwillingness to share with others. ("I rarely get anything worthwhile, so why should I share it? I'm going to keep it all for me.")

> Blaming others for difficulties and problems. ("Others try to make my life hard.")

> Rejecting spiritual teachings that could help. ("God isn't loving or he wouldn't allow this to happen. I don't believe in God.")[30]

7. When depressed teens speak, they're negative about themselves and everything in their life. They draw conclusions based on their negative mind-set rather than on fact. This further reinforces their feelings of depression.

8. Depressed teens will show unusual levels of frustration and irritability. When they fail to reach their goals, they'll be especially hard on themselves, commenting disparagingly about their abilities and value.

9. Depressed teens look for comfort and support from others, but when they receive it, they refuse to be comforted and encouraged.

10. Some teens will mask their feelings of despair by clowning and acting foolish. Provocative teens are less likely to appear in need of comfort and support, so the depression can continue undetected.

11. Some demonstrate drastic mood swings when depressed. One minute they appear to be "up" and the next minute they're in the pit of despair. These teens tend to believe that if they are "good" enough and work hard enough that life will turn around for them.

12. The depressed adolescent may become the family scapegoat. The teen's behavior can elicit anger and parents might label him or her "a problem child." With this label, the depression continues and the teen may begin to live up to this classification.

13. They may tend to be passive and excessively dependent and assume parents automatically know their needs. Since it's impossible to read all their thoughts, their needs go unmet. They may become angry and respond in passive aggressive ways.

14. Depressed teens tend to be overly sensitive, hard on themselves, and self-critical. They create unreasonable goals for themselves and blame themselves when they fail to attain them.

15. Some depressed teens will regress (show childish behaviors from the past) or become obsessive in order to cope with how badly they feel.

Reasons for Teen Depression

Many teens experience depression because they are having difficulties dealing with other people. The strongest need most teens have is to belong—to be part of a family and social group. Adolescents who are having problems developing positive relationships are in crisis and can become depressed.

Depression can also result from a traumatic incident. In such cases, the depressed feelings are often short-lived; the depression may lift, but not the trauma symptoms. The following are situations that may not be bothersome to adults, but they can cause temporary depression in teens:

> Failing an exam or a class

> Being overlooked for a desired position

> Performing poorly in an organized activity such as team sports or gymnastics, or getting cut from a team

> Unable to find someone with whom to hang out with

> Being reprimanded or punished

> Arguing with a parent, sibling, or friend

> Losing a favorite object or a pet

> Being denied a request

> Entering puberty

> Moving from one home to another or losing friends

> Not hitting a much-wanted goal

ELEVEN WAYS TO HELP YOUR DEPRESSED TEEN

Most parents don't know what to do for their depressed teen. What can you say to your depressed teenager?

Thirteen-year-old Katy begins to cry at the drop of a hat. She constantly makes negative statements about herself. She talks about being ugly (which is far from the truth), how others don't like her (her friends call her everyday), and how she can't do anything right (she is a straight-A student). This has been going on for a month. No matter what her parents say or do, she seems to get worse rather than better. How should Katy's parents respond to her? What can they say to her? What can they do to help Katy get through this time?

Your teen is not trying to punish you.

A good place to start is by communicating that they care for Katy, want to be with her, and will be available to her. Conveying acceptance is also important. There is a healing in physical touch. An arm around your teen's shoulder, a pat on the back, or holding your teenager's hand can communicate comfort and acceptance. But by all means, be honest and tell your teen, "I don't really understand all that you're going through, but I'm trying—and I'm here to help you."

Here are some practical suggestions to help you understand and deal with the problem of depression.

How closely you follow these will depend upon the intensity and duration of the depression. If your teen is experiencing short-term depression and still functioning, certain suggestions will not apply. However, if the depression has lasted quite a while and your teen is not eating, sleeping, or functioning on a normal level, apply more of these guidelines to the situation.

1. Help Your Teen Learn to Express Depressed Feelings

Keep in mind that depression robs people of the ability to govern their thinking and emotions. If your depressed teen just stares, ignores greetings, or turns away from you, remember that he or she doesn't want to act that way. Your teen is not trying to punish you. Severely depressed teens can't control themselves any more than you could walk a straight line after twirling around twenty-five times.

When they do begin to talk about their feelings, several important guidelines should be followed:

➤ Your nonverbal expressions should indicate a

genuine interest in what your teen is saying. Avoid anything that might distract you from focusing directly on your teenager.

➤ Use questions to gather information from your teen.

➤ Withhold giving your opinions, information, or advice until your teen is ready and open for assistance.

➤ Control your own emotions. It will help your teen maintain his or her composure. A power struggle at this point could serve to just intensify your teen's feelings.

➤ Don't try to fill every moment with words. Silence can allow teens to organize their thoughts.

➤ Watch your teen's nonverbal expressions. Look for the feelings that lie beneath your teen's words.

➤ Allow for disagreement. Your child's perspective may be different from yours.[31]

2. Watch Out for the Possibility of Suicide

The family of a depressed teen should be aware of the possibility of suicide. It may shock you, but any suspicions of suicide should be taken seriously. Unfortunately, the incidence of suicide is on the rise, and a teen who expresses utter hopelessness for the future may be at risk, If your teen is able to talk about his or her suicidal thoughts or plans, help bring them out into the open as well as offer your support and help.

3. Consult with Your Doctor

Certain physical problems can cause feelings of depression. When a teen suffers from long-term depression, it's important to consult your doctor for possible causes and treatments.

4. Give Support and Make Adjustments

The whole family needs to be informed and coached when your teen is depressed. Ask each person to avoid conflicts, put-downs, and unrealistic expectations until things are back to normal. Confrontation and strong discipline should be suspended until stability is restored.

5. Don't Avoid the Depressed Teen

Avoiding depressed teens further isolates them and worsens the problem. Don't allow yourself to feel guilty, as if you were responsible for the depression.

6. Realize That a Depressed Teen Is a Hurting Teen

Don't tell a depressed teen, "Just snap out of it." Avoid offering simple solutions ("Just pray about it." "Read your Bible more.") And never imply that your teen is using depression to solicit sympathy. Don't criticize your teen for a lack of faith in God.

7. Empathize rather than Sympathize with Your Teen

Empathy is feeling *with* your teen. It's as though you're in the driver's seat with him or her, feeling and sensing the same things.

It's putting Galatians 6:2 and Romans 12:15 into practice:

> *Carry each other's burdens, and in this way you will fulfill the law of Christ.*
>
> — Galatians 6:2

> *Rejoice with those who rejoice; mourn with those who mourn.*
>
> Romans 12:15

Sympathy ("Oh, you poor thing!") only reinforces someone's feelings of hopelessness. If you've gone through depression or a long period of disappointment or loss, share it.

8. Reconstruct Your Teen's Self-Esteem

One of the most important steps you can take is to help your teen build his or her self-esteem, because when depression occurs, self-esteem tends to crumble. Depressed teens don't understand their value as God's creation and the extent of God's love for them. Because of this, they doubt everyone's love as well.

9. Watch Your Teen's Diet

A depressed teen may have no appetite, but nutrition is still important. Don't let food become another issue by harping on it or using guilt to get your teen to eat. Just provide nourishing food.

10. Keep Your Teen Busy Physically

To the severely depressed teen, physical activity is more beneficial than mental activity. Your teen's behavior — avoiding others, withdrawing from normal activities, not eating well, and offending friends—will tend to reinforce his or her depression. For this reason, you may run into resistance, so you'll need to take charge of planning your teen's activities.

11. Never Tease or Belittle Your Teen for a Lack of Self-Confidence

Neither showcase nor ignore your teen's low self-esteem. It is a common problem of depression and must be faced. Don't argue about or participate in your teen's self-pity, but present the illogical nature of his or her self-disparagement.

CHAPTER FOUR

Interacting with Your Teens

N o matter what is happening with your teen, you need to connect with him or her as a parent. And part of that connection involves guidance through a set of rules.

How do you set limits with your teens? Do you really need a set of rules? You both need them. Parenting means guidance—giving help and structure to help the teens function. Your teens need your parenting, which includes rules. Sometimes when teens struggle, parents tend to give too much freedom or not reinforce the rules previously established. But rules and limits are important for the sense of security adolescents feel, even though they may not like the rules or may break them.[32]

FOUR BASIC PRINCIPLES OF RULES

Regardless of the rules you set down for your teens, four basic principles must be followed.

1. A Rule Should Be Definable

If a rule is well-defined, teens will know instantly when they have broken it. It must be so specifically presented that all concerned know what is actually meant by the rule.

Some parents are not as explicit as they should be and expect their teenagers to be mind readers. Many a parent has said, "Well, he ought to know that's what I meant." Telling your daughter she cannot go somewhere until her room is clean may sound explicit, but it is a poorly defined rule because it doesn't tell specifically what is expected (dusting? straightening? vacuuming?).

2. A Rule Should Be Reasonable

Any rule should actually make the environment more comfortable for your teens. When they follow the rules, they are performing normal, necessary functions. Make sure that teens are capable of following the rules you establish.

3. A Rule Should Be Enforceable

Whenever a rule is stated, anticipate that it may be broken. Most teens like to test rules. If you cannot enforce a rule consistently, you cannot expect them to follow it. How do you know whether or not a rule can be enforced? Determine whether you are capable of knowing every time they break the rule without depending on another person's testimony. You must be able to find out easily whether a rule has been broken.

4. A Rule Should Help a Person Develop Inner Values and Control

The rule will eventually help a teen become an independent, responsible person. The rule should be for the benefit of the parent as well as for the benefit of your teen and others.

HOW TO FOSTER COOPERATION

How can parents help their adolescents stay out of trouble without controlling them? Consider the following suggestions:

1. Regular times should be established for family discussion.

These may take place at the dinner table, while driving to or from school, during a walk after dinner, or whenever you can establish a pattern. It also means being available when your teens have a need to share.

2. Let your teenagers know you want to hear what they have to say.

This means there will be times when you *will not* share your opinion or expertise on the subject. You may consider some thoughts to be way off base. (They may think the same of some of yours). You may want to "set them straight"; but unless you let them express their ideas without fear of being jumped on, they will learn not to say anything at all.

It is difficult to remain silent when your teens hold views contrary to your own. Most parents want teenagers to accept their ideas and opinions. Yet to develop their thinking ability, teens need to learn to explore ideas and beliefs. You may not agree with what they say, and you have a right to explain your opposing viewpoint. But you both can discuss opinions calmly, in a proper tone of voice, with courtesy toward each other.

3. Set limits on behavior but not on opinions.

This is perhaps the most difficult guideline for parents to carry out without becoming overly threatened. A free expression of opinion, with proper rules of courtesy, is one of the healthiest goals a family can work toward. The effort will create an atmosphere in which people learn to listen to one another.

4. Always encourage your teenagers.

We all need to be encouraged. We need to know that we are okay, that we count, and that our efforts (not necessarily results) are recognized and appreciated. Affirm your teens for who they are as individual people.

5. Your teenagers need to be responsible for what they do.

Do not let them blame others for their own actions. I remember a situation one night when a seventeen-year-old arrived home more than an hour late from his date. Both of his parents were still up. They simply looked at him with a wondering expression as he walked in. He started to say, "Sorry I'm late, but that dumb car ran out of gas." But halfway through he stopped, grinned, and said, "Nope. I'm late because I neglected to take the time to put some gas in the car, so I'm the culprit." The parents gave a small grin and one said, "Thanks. We both appreciate your telling us that." And they said no more. They did not have to remind him to put gas in the car next time. He learned through his experience. His remark demonstrated the benefits of some well-spent discussion times with his parents as he was growing into adolescence.

6. Teenagers have to learn to accept the consequences for what they do.

Allowing them to experience the logical and natural consequences of their actions provides honest and real learning situations.

A friend of mine told of a procedure he used that has worked for several other families with teenagers who are dating. When this man's daughter went out on a date, she was expected home at a certain time. When she was fifteen, she had to be in at 11:00; at sixteen, 11:30; and at seventeen, 12:00. A few exceptions were made for special occasions. She knew that if she came in half an hour late, she would have to make up that half hour by coming home much earlier on the next date. Whether it was five minutes or an hour, it was made up on the next date, regardless of the occasion. Very little discussion was needed; the rule was established with its natural consequence and everyone knew what it was.

7. As was suggested earlier, let your teenagers make choices.

"John, you will have to make a decision. You can go to Jim's house this evening to work on your car and then fix the garage door tomorrow night, or you can do the reverse. You make the choice, and I'll go along with it." Many potentially explosive encounters between parents and teenagers can be defused when parents approach their teens with several possible choices. Sometimes teenagers may counter with an additional choice, which may be a valid possibility. You will have to decide whether or not to allow that alternative.

QUESTIONS FOR CONVERSATION[33]

You can use the following questions with your teens to develop a conversation. Be sure to listen carefully. If you don't agree with what your teens say or believe, don't react or correct, or your teens may not respond at all the next time.

If your teens ask you what you believe about the same question, try to match the length of your answer with their answer. This is not the time for lecturing or giving an earful.

Use the questions sparingly and try to weave them into everyday conversations. Sometimes parents think they know what their teens are thinking; instead, ask them and let them speak for themselves. You may be surprised.

1. What are three things you like about your best friend?

2. If you could live anywhere else, where would it be?

3. What's the best time of the day for you? What's the worst time?

4. What do you wish your teacher would do differently?

5. If you could change one thing about this house, what would it be?

6. If you could ask God three questions, what would they be?

7. When you read something, do you see pictures of it in your brain or do you hear the words?

8. What do you remember most from five years ago?

9. What do you want to do five years from now?

10. What makes it easy to talk to others?

11. What were two of the questions on your test today?

12. What angers or upsets you the most at school?

13. What angers or upsets you the most at home?

14. What do you like and dislike the most at church?

15. What do you like most about the way you look?

16. What do you dislike the most about the way you look?

17. Most of us have things we worry about. What do you worry about?

18. How often does bullying happen in your school?

19. What kind of clothes do you wish you could wear?

20. I need your advice on something. What do you think about . . .?

21. What do you think I could do so that we could talk better together (or get better)?

22. What do you think about the time of your bedtime (or curfew)?

23. Did I ever tell you about my first date?

24. Did I ever tell you about my first kiss?

25. Did I ever tell you about the time I was sent to the principal's office?

26. When you hear that someone died, what do you think?

27. World Trade Center: What goes through your mind?

28. When you hear that a friend's parents are divorcing, what do you think?

29. What do you wish Jesus would do today?

30. What do you think about drinking alcohol?

31. What's the main reason your friends drink?

32. Do you think there are many kids at your school who use drugs?

33. What's it like for you when you succeed?

34. What's it like for you when you fail?

35. What do you wish we would do when you fail?

36. What's the hardest feeling for you to put into words?

37. How do you see others treating those who are gay?

38. What's the best thing about the Internet?

39. What's the worst thing you've seen on the Internet?

40. If you could play a musical instrument (or an additional instrument), what would it be?

41. In what way do you feel pressure from your friends?

42. There's a lot of sex on TV, in movies, and on the Internet. What do you think about sex in the media?

43. What do you appreciate most about your pastor (or youth leader)?

44. What don't you appreciate about your pastor (or youth leader)?

45. Who would you say is a hero in your life?

46. When you drive, what will be your biggest concern?

47. What do you think about smoking?

48. What are the reasons to smoke or not to smoke?

49. Do you know what stresses you the most?

50. What's the best thing that's happened to you this year?

51. What do you think when you see someone who has a lot of body piercings?

52. Have you ever thought about getting a tattoo?

53. Have you ever asked your tattooed or pierced friends to tell you about their experiences before and after the procedure?

54. If you could ask either of us any question you ever wanted to ask, what would it be?

Discussing these questions may help your teens during the difficult times in their lives.

THE PROMISE OF A RAINBOW

Adolescence is often a stormy time. Storms come in all kinds of intensities. In your life, the storm may be a dramatic one—a teen running away, getting involved in drugs or alcohol, being sexually promiscuous, joining a cult, changing his or her sexual orientation, among a host of other behaviors.[34] Or your cause for concern may be more like a slow, steady rain, eroding the foundation you have so carefully laid for your teens' lives—a persistent lack of effort at school, no desire to attend church functions, a preference for deadbeat friends. Either way, the result is the same: inside, you feel shattered.

It could be your teen is a *prodigal*. Not a pleasant term. It leaves a bad taste in your mouth and a sinking feeling in the pit of your stomach. It's a label given to people who are wasteful. But it's not just money some teens waste. It's the value system you've been trying to instill. It's their potential, their abilities,

> There will be a day when you'll see a rainbow again.

their health, perhaps even their lives. It's upsetting to you, but in many cases, they really don't care. When teens become prodigals, dreams are tarnished. Sometimes they're not just damaged, they're shattered. Some are kept faintly alive like the smoldering coals of a fire; others die. It's a difficult to say which is hardest.

Where do you go from here? You'd probably like to get out of the storms that disrupt your life. But like a rainstorm or a blizzard, there's no real way to know when this storm will end. Storms are a part of nature. They're also part of our lives. There is hope, however. I once heard someone say, "When you're in a thunderstorm, always look for the rainbow."

There were three men in the Bible who saw rainbows. One was Noah, who saw the rainbow *after* the storm. Like him, there will be a day in the future when you'll see a rainbow again. Count on that.

Ezekiel saw the rainbow in the midst of the storm. Even though he and the other Jews had been exiled to Babylon and even though Jerusalem and the temple were about to be destroyed, he knew by the rainbow that God was still there. You can't ignore your storm, but you can look for the rainbow. It's there.

In Revelation 4, John saw the rainbow *before* the storm. He saw a complete circle, not just the bow. It meant that God would be in control before, during, and after the storm he was learning about.

Hear these words from a message by a retired missionary who experienced many storms in life:

You and I will experience storms until we are called to heaven; and then all storms will cease. Expect the storms and don't be afraid of them, because God is always faithful. Just remember God's message to us today: *Always look for the rainbow.* Depend on the faithfulness of God. Sometimes he'll show you the rainbow after the storm, sometimes during the storm, and sometimes before the storm. *But he will never fail you.* [35]

Notes

1   Don H. Fontanelle, *Keys to Parenting Your Teenager* (Hauppauge, NY: Baron's Educational Series, 2000), p. 8.

2   Barbara C. Unell and Jerry Wyckoff, *The Eight Seasons of Parenthood* 1st ed. (Crown, 2000).

3   Jay Kesler with Ronald A. Beers, *Parents and Teenagers* (Wheaton, IL: Victor Books, 1984) p. 17.

4   Les Parrott III, *Helping the Struggling Adolescence: A Guide to Thirty-six Common Problems for Counselors, Pastors, and Youth* (Grand Rapids MI: Zondervan, 2000), pp. 18–21.

5   Much of this section is from H. Norman Wright, *The Complete Guide to Crisis and Trauma Counseling: What to Do and Say When It Matters Most!* (Ventura, CA: Regal Books, 2011), chapter 13.

6   G. Keith Olson, *Counseling Teenagers: The Complete Christian Guide to Understanding and Helping Adolescents* (Loveland, CO: Group Books, 1984), pp. 27-28.

7   Ibid., pp. 55-56.

8   William Van Ornum and John B. Mordock, *Crisis Counseling with Children and Adolescents: A Guide for Nonprofessional Counselors* (New York: Continuum, 1983), pp. 41-43.

9   Much of the following information originally appeared in Wright, *The Complete Guide to Crisis and Trauma Counseling*, chapter 4.

10   Ibid., chapter 10.

11   Judith K. Acosta and Richard L. Levenson, Jr., "Observations from Ground Zero at the World Trade Center in New York City, Part II: Theoretical and Clinical Considerations," *International Journal of Emergency Mental Health* 4, no. 2 (Spring 2002), pp. 120–21.

12 For additional information on trauma, see H. Norman Wright and Matt Woodley and Julie Woodley, *Finding Hope When Life Goes Wrong* (Grand Rapids, MI: Revell, 2008).

13 Richard Heyman, *How to Say It to Teens: Talking about the Most Important Topics of Their Lives* (Paramus, NJ: Prentice Hall Press, 2001), pp. 36–37.

14 Ibid., p. 138.

15 Mary Ann Emswiler and James P. Emswiler, *Guiding Your Child through Grief* (New York: Bantam Books, 2000), p. 159.

16 Heyman, *How to Say It to Teens*, pp. 104–105.

17 Much of this section is from Wright, *The Complete Guide to Crisis and Trauma Counseling*, chapter 18.

18 Carol Staudacher, *Beyond Grief: A Guide for Recovering from the Death of a Loved One* (Oakland, CA: New Harbinger Publications, 1987), p. 129.

19 The section is based on Staudacher, *Beyond Grief*, pp. 131–38.

20 Dan Schaefer and Christine Lyons, *How Do We Tell the Children? A Parents' Guide to Helping Children Understand and Cope When Someone Dies* (New York: Newmarket Press: 1986), p. 129.

21 Find BlobTree communication tools at www.blobtree.com (Copyright © pip wilson and Ian Long from 'Games without Frontiers')

22 Staudacher, *Beyond Grief*, pp. 146–47.

23 Joanne T. Jozefowski, *The Phoenix Phenomenon: Rising from the Ashes of Grief* (Northvale, NJ: Jason Aronson, Inc., 2001), p. 17.

24 Staudacher, *Beyond Grief*, p. 151.

25 Wright, *The Complete Guide to Crisis and Trauma Counseling*, pp. 7–8.

26 Therese A. Rando, *Grieving: How to Go On Living When Someone You Love Dies* (Lexington, MA: Lexington Books, 1988), adapted p. 215.

27 Ibid.

28 Staudacher, *Beyond Grief*, pp. 138–39.

29 Material in the rest of this chapter originally appeared in H. Norman Wright, *Helping Your Kids Deal with Anger, Fear, and Sadness* (Eugene, OR: Harvest House Publishers, 2005), pp. 123–48.

30 Frederic F. Flach and Suzanne C. Draghi, eds., *The Nature and Treatment of Depression* (New York: John Wiley and Sons, Inc., 1975), pp. 89-90.

31 William Lee Carter, *Kid Think* (Dallas, TX: Rapha Publishing, 1992), p. 129.

32 For more detailed information about how to talk to teens about important topics, see Richard Heyman, *How to Say It to Teens: Talking About the Most Important Topics of Their Lives* (Paramus, NJ: Prentice Hall Press, 2001).

33 This section is from H. Norman Wright, How to Talk So Your Kids Will Listen: From Toddlers to Teenagers: Connecting with Your Children at Every Age (Bethany House Publishers, 2004).

34 For detailed information on coping with teen storms and the struggles of tough situations, see H. Norman Wright, *Loving Your Rebellious Child: A Survival Guide for Parents of Prodigals* (Franklin, TN: Authentic Publishers, 2013).

35 Warren W. Wiersbe, *Preaching and Teaching with Imagination; The Quest for Biblical Ministry* (Grand Rapids, MI: Baker Books, 1994), p. 59.